M000087444

HOW TO REPORT UNSCHOOLING TO SCHOOL OFFICIALS

HOW TO REPORT UNSCHOOLING TO SCHOOL OFFICIALS

Patrick Farenga

Excerpts from *Teach Your Own* and *Growing Without Schooling* are used with the author's permission.

Printed in the United States of America
HoltGWS LLC, 13 Hume Avenue, Medford, MA 02155

ISBN-10: 0985400226
ISBN-13: 978-0-9854002-2-4

There's an old story about two men on a train. One of them, seeing some naked-looking sheep in a field, said, "Those sheep have been sheared." The other looked a moment longer, and then said, "They seem to be—on this side." It is in such a cautious spirit that we should say whatever we have to say about the working of the mind.

—John Holt, *How Children Learn*

Not everything that can be counted counts, and not everything that counts can be counted. —Albert Einstein

CONTENTS

INTRODUCTION

Writing a report about doing school at home is easier in many ways than writing one about unschooling, since you will have many of the conventional products of schooling to share with school officials, such as tests, worksheets, and commonly used textbooks. Unschooling often doesn't produce such products, so if your state requires you to submit a periodic evaluation (and not all states require this, so check your local homeschooling laws or regulations) you might need to explain your children's growth and development in more depth to readers who do not understand unschooling. This book will help you do this, but I don't want you to get uptight about reporting to school officials, so I'll outline the basic steps here so you can see it isn't as complicated as you might think.

1) Collect and review your journals, notes, documents, videos, photos, and other records of your children's education efforts for the year. If none exist, create an after-the-fact curriculum, where you and your children look back over your year and recreate on paper what you did. Remember as unschoolers our philosophy is, as John Holt wrote, we are learning all the time—everything your child does counts as learning. For purposes of reporting to school, unschooling means learning without following any school's

curriculum. Unschoolers use real-life experiences to grow and learn, using school methods as needed, if at all.

2) With your child, discuss what to report to the school that you think best represents their efforts for the year. You should have some evidence to back up your report if the school decides it needs to better understand what you are doing (written work, photos of projects and team efforts, recommendations from other adults your children study or work with, and so on).

3) Write in plain English the things your child did during the year and put them into broad subject categories that mesh with your educational plans. I think it is a good idea to state that unschooling is your educational philosophy at the beginning of the report to contextualize your children's learning. This helps if your child is below school's grade level for their age—such as a child who learns to read at an older age than they do in school (typically 9 years old in most U.S. public schools)—this is due to unschooling and not educational neglect.

You don't need to dress up common events into school jargon unless you think it will help you communicate better with the school ("educationese" gets discussed at length later in this booklet). In fact, I recommend giving the school only what it needs to determine if sufficient educational progress has occurred and no more. Some people feel they need to prove their seriousness as educators by closely detailing their efforts in their reports, but this isn't necessary. First, doing so can backfire and cause the school to pressure other parents to provide more details than the law asks because "Mr. Jones has no problem telling us how much algebra he made his children do." Second, the schools do not usually read these reports closely; they want the paperwork primarily for their files and regulatory compliance, not for its content. You will not get a commendation from the school board for writing an incredibly detailed homeschooling report.

However, there is a very good reason for keeping careful records of your children's learning—for your family's personal use. Years ago, a friend of mine, Elsa Haas, started homeschooling her son when he would have entered first grade in New York City. New York requires quarterly reports from homeschoolers, and Elsa eventually became frustrated by bureaucratic bungling regarding her reports. But Elsa enjoyed keeping, reflecting, and sharing her observations about her son's learning, so she decided to keep her detailed journal and culled a short quarterly report for school from it. Cleverly, Elsa left ellipses throughout her abridged reports and openly invited the authorities to read the unabridged versions. Over a decade of reports later, the authorities never asked to read Elsa's unabridged reports.

The main thing is to honestly report as unschooling the learning your child does during the year; there's no need to be ashamed because they haven't learned to play the oboe or mastered calculus as other homeschoolers the same age may do. As you read this booklet you will see that the world outside of school provides more than enough "curricular material" for children to learn and grow into competent adults and citizens.

UNSCHOOLING AND THE SCHOOLS

Homeschooling is the overall legal term for getting documented as a family that learns outside of school without being considered truant. So you need to notify the school authorities that you are homeschooling first, then describe unschooling as your method in your homeschooling plan (Note: most, but not all, states require you to submit a homeschooling plan and subsequent reports. Be sure to research your state's homeschooling laws or regulations to see if you must do this paperwork.) Unschooling is the process that allows your children the time and space to determine what, when, how, why, and from whom they want to learn. As a process, unschooling can accelerate individual achievement or take some time—even years—to reproduce the conventional results of school learning. Research on unschoolers and alternative schoolers (see Appendix 1) show that children who don't learn by using any standard school curriculum in elementary or high school are nonetheless learning (known as self-directed learning) and, if needed, these students can learn whatever they missed when they are older.

Unschooling is not like conventional school, where the time and space for each student's learning is controlled, predicted, and evaluated by professional teachers on a daily basis. School uses a fixed curriculum to determine children's learning, expecting certain test results after classroom lessons, and then remediating as they see fit. Unschooling focuses on a child's social-emotional learning (SEL) and real-world experiences rather than test scores to determine outcomes and next steps. This is a reason John Holt, who promoted the concept of unschooling, named the magazine he founded *Growing Without Schooling*: you don't have to go to school to grow into a competent adult. Unschooling is unique for each child, so it needs a different evaluation method to capture the scope and sequence of self-directed learning.

Unschooling may be a new word to describe learning but it is not an unheard of concept in education, and there are public and private schools that use it. Free schools, open classrooms, Sudbury Valley Schools, independent alternative schools, experiential learning programs, and other alternatives for students who don't do well in standardized schools have been around as long as conventional schools. A famous alternative school run by its students, Summerhill in England, was founded in 1921 and is still producing graduates today, without ever using standard grades, tests, and curricula.

Educators acknowledge that one-size-fits-all learning is not for everyone, which is why private schools can develop their own teaching and learning processes—such as Reggio Emilia, Montessori, and Waldorf schools—and why some of these private schools are used as models for public school reforms. Further, many public school teachers are now forgoing the conventional textbook-and-testing model and are customizing their lessons using chunks of curricula from various sources.[1] Unschooling lets parents pick and choose whatever method, or bits of curricula, they want to use with their children, and they can evaluate their children's progress without grades and scores, just as some public and private schools do.[2]

It is also important to remember that no state in the United States requires a homeschooling parent to have a public school teaching certificate, just as many private schools do not require one (though some, such as Montessori and Waldorf, require teacher training in their unique programs).

The main thing to remember is you and your children can pick and choose experiences, tutors, friends, classes (online or in buildings), books, materials, sports activities, hobbies, and so on

---

[1] Molnar, Michelle. 2015. "Companies Face Rising Demand for Bite-Size Chunks of Curricula." *Education Week.* June 10, 2015. http://www.edweek.org/ew/articles/2015/06/11/companies-face-rising-demand-for-bite-size-chunks.html.

[2] For example, see "Gradeless Schools: Exploring Alternative Evaluation Methods," by Kathryn DeBros. Feb. 20, 2015. *Noodle.com.* https://www.noodle.com/articles/school-without-grades-alternative-assessment-beyond-gpas. See, too, the Badass Teachers Association on Facebook, and other teacher-organized groups, as evidence that not all professional educators view testing and grading as vital to their ability to teach children.

that have meaning and purpose to your child *now*. You don't have to use the Common Core or other standard curricula; as long as your children learn to read, write, and calculate it won't matter how and where they learned to do so.

Every state has a compulsory school law, which means children must attend a school or prove that they are being otherwise educated, not that they all must learn the same thing at the same time. That's why a variety of public and private schools exist and why homeschooling is allowed in the United States and many other countries.

CURRICULA

If you're worried about whether your unschooled children are at or below a particular grade level in public school, or if you just want to know what kids in school are learning who are the same age as your unschooled children, you can check out these course outlines for most U.S. public schools using Worldbook Encyclopedia's *Typical Course of Study, K through 12* [http://www.worldbook.com/free-educational-resources/typical-course-of-study]. Worldbook notes:

> The lists are compiled from an overview of the following: requirements/standards as outlined by states; the recommended expectations/standards from recognized, respected organizations in each field; and the expectations identified in major textbooks for each subject and grade level. The lists focus on those expectations that are most common across the states and sources. While any one list won't fit any one locale exactly, it will give a realistic picture of the kinds of academic skills and understandings a child that age should have and is actually expected (by their schools) to have.

Here are some other resources you can use to see what children are expected to learn in different grades, and to see how varied the scopes and sequences of school curricula are.

- E.D. Hirsch, *What Every First Grader Needs to Know* (The Core Knowledge curriculum):
  - o http://www.coreknowledge.org/about-the-curriculum
- Inspired by Mortimer Adler's Great Books curriculum: [www.britannica.com/biography/Mortimer-J-Adler]:
  - o The Great Books Curriculum (K—12 example): http://greatbooksacademy.org/curriculum/
  - o High school and college example: http://www.nationalgreatbooks.com/
- Waldorf School Curriculum:
  www.whywaldorfworks.org/02_w_education/curriculum.asp
- Montessori School Curriculum:
  www.montessori-icme.com/method.html

The large homeschooling curriculum market further displays a rich variety that families can choose from if they want a school-at-home situation, including diagnostic and achievement testing of children that parents can purchase. Just creating the preceding list undermines the idea that there must be one path to learn that everyone must follow. Indeed, though John Holt is talking about homeschooling in the following statement from 1981 (reproduced in full in Appendix 2), it is very applicable to our general education situation in 2015, since education is available in even more forms and media. John Holt was part of a panel on the Committee on Education of the Massachusetts State legislature in 1981 and he summarized the Constitutional basis of homeschooling. Here are pertinent excerpts to keep in your mind that support your choice to unschool if you report to school officials.

> . . . The U.S. Constitution, under the First, Ninth, and Fourteenth Amendments, protects the rights of parents to get for the children the kind of education they want.
> . . . The Supreme Court, in *Pierce v Society of Sisters* (1925) and *Farrington v. Tokushige* (1927), in upholding this right, said that the states could not, either through laws or regulations, impose a uniform system of education on all children.
> . . . Where the Supreme Court has upheld that the states have the legal power, under the Constitution, to regulate the education of children, it has done so on this ground alone,

that the people have a right to protect themselves against the danger that uneducated children might grow up so ignorant as to be unemployable and a burden to the state . . .

. . . It might even be helpful to make clear, by resolution or amendment to the existing education statutes, that the intent of the compulsory education laws is not to empower the state or the several school districts to impose a uniform system of education on all parents. [Emphasis added by me—PF].

Unschooling shows you don't need to choose *any* curriculum to help children learn. You help your children learn as human beings have done throughout history: By paying attention to their interests and growth, their words and actions, they show you how to best help them learn. You may use a class, textbook, or mentor, but you are doing so on an as-needed basis, not as a compulsory obligation.

RECORDKEEPING

There are two types of recordkeeping homeschoolers can do: that which is required by the state, and that which they want to do for themselves. Of course, there is some overlap, but on the whole these are very different types of records. States, and in some cases local school districts, vary in the amount and the kind of record keeping they require of homeschoolers. The first thing you want to do is find out what you have to do legally. Some states require testing (but not always every year); some allow parents to choose among testing, keeping a portfolio, or writing up reports; and some states don't require testing or much recordkeeping at all. In about nine states, as of this writing, homeschoolers must formally write up their curriculum and submit it to their local education authorities. In other states, requirements are less extensive, so be sure to check the homeschooling laws or regulations in your state.

No matter what your state's requirements, you can find a way to fulfill them without getting bogged down or worrying more than is necessary about how much your children are accomplishing. In any case, whether or not your state has recordkeeping requirements, you may find, as many parents do, that you want to keep some kind of record of your homeschooling, for your own peace of mind and for the fun of chronicling your child's growth— just as parents have always saved their children's drawings, stories, projects, and so on.

Katharine Houk, a longtime homeschooler from New York, wrote to *Growing Without Schooling* about several ways to keep records:

A topic that frequently comes up at homeschooling support-group meetings at the beginning of the homeschool year is record keeping. For those of us whose homeschooling approach is interest-initiated and far-ranging, it can be a challenge to write quarterly reports for submission to the school district, when learning is expected to be pigeonholed into subject areas.

When our family first started homeschooling, the New York State Home Instruction Regulation was not in effect. Homeschooling was permitted, but was handled differently by each school district, with guidelines from the State Education Department offering suggestions on how to handle homeschooling. Our district gave us a checklist to fill out periodically, and that was the extent of our reporting. But at that time, I kept daily logs of my children's activities, even though I didn't need them for reporting purposes. I was fascinated with their learning processes, and had great fun documenting all the wonderful things they did. Most of their learning was through play; they played intensely, happily, and for hours and days at a time. My challenge was in translating their activities and our conversations and experiences into a form that would fit in the subject area boxes in my logbook.

When the need for reporting came along, with the passage of the current regulation, it was easy for us to make that transition; we had already been keeping records. Besides the requirement that as homeschoolers you must keep an attendance record (!), there is no specific requirement for record keeping in the regulation. But I knew that having a written record of our activities would be helpful to me in writing reports. Besides, I was already in the habit of doing it, and enjoyed creating a record of my children's learning. I used a loose-leaf notebook for each child. In the front were pages that looked like a lesson plan book, with subject areas listed down the left side of the page, and the days of the week

across the top of the page. I included Saturday
and Sunday, because learning doesn't stop for
weekends. In the notebook I also included a
place to record field trips and keep
photographs, pocket pages for papers, etc. It
served us well, and the children enjoy looking
back at them, laughing at the spelling in their
early writings, and reminiscing about trips
and other activities from years ago. As the
children grew older, I grew weary of sifting
their learning into subject area categories.
Their learning is all of a piece, and it became
tedious to chop it up into artificial
compartments on a daily basis. Therefore I
changed the notebook to include lined paper,
where each day I would write a few sentences
about what was done that day. At the end of
each month I would make a synopsis of the
month by subject area. Then when it came
time for a quarterly report I would have
something to work from.

Now that the children are so much older
(12 and 15), it is unnecessary for me alone to
do all the record keeping. Also, my offspring
are such independent learners and I am so

busy that often I am not aware of their activities or of what books they are reading. I do jot things down from time to time that I am aware of and that I find especially noteworthy, but I ask each of them to keep their own notebook, and to write down the books they are reading and their activities, plus whatever else they care to put in their journals. This way I am not invading their privacy, and they have a record in their own writing of what they have done. At report time, they share with us the parts of their journals that they want in their reports. Privacy is an important issue, one that is sometimes not taken into account when school districts want to know everything that is happening with our children. Some families I know use a spiral-bound notebook for record keeping, and store papers in a separate portfolio. Also there are commercially distributed record-keeping systems you can purchase. Whatever method of record keeping you choose, the results will help you in writing reports and complying with assessment requirements, and will be a wonderful chronicle of your children's growth and development.

Documentation Ideas for Older Unschoolers

Since compulsory school age ends at age 16 in many states (but check your compulsory school law—it is being raised to 18 in many states as I write), there is no legal or regulatory reason to keep sending the school your reports after that age. However, since getting into college requires a high school transcript and diploma or its equivalent, I want to provide some basic information for reporting unschooling during the high school years. High school documentation is important to do if you want to create a transcript for college admission. There are schools and services that will provide transcripts and high school diplomas for a fee, but many people unschool through the high school years and get into higher education without paying others to help them. Here are three resources that will help you do this.

If you want a more detailed presentation about record keeping and evaluations for homeschoolers, particularly for high school records and college admissions, I recommend Loretta Heuer's comprehensive book *The Homeschooler's Guide to Portfolios and Transcripts* [http://amzn.to/1fEf7tY].

A recently revised and superb book about creating high school transcripts for college admission or employment is *Self-*

Directed Learning; Documentation and Life Stories by Wes Beach [www.giftedhomeschoolers.org, 2015].

The Art of Self-Directed Learning [http://amzn.to/1IPkFia], by Blake Boles is very useful for teenagers who want to follow their own intrinsic motivations for learning; it is good for parents to read, too, so they can better understand what self-directed learning looks and feels like, and how it produces different results than what they probably expect from a conventional high school. Boles' other books and websites about unschooling and teenagers are well worth reading, too [www.blakeboles.com/].

EVALUATIONS

John Holt and I write in _Teach Your Own_ about the value of providing authentic feedback to students versus a grade and why homeschoolers don't need grades to evaluate progress and plan their next steps. To explain why this is so, I'll use John's words about evaluations in and out of school from an earlier book he wrote, _What Do I Do Monday?_ (currently out of print).

> In the kind of learning I have been talking about there is no place and no need for conventional testing and grading. In a class where children are doing things, and not getting ready to do them sometime in the distant future, what they do tells us what they have learned. What sense does an average grade make in a course like English? Do we average a serious writer's best work against his worst? If I assigned a paper, and a student did badly on it, this only showed that this was the wrong paper for him, where he could not show the ability he had. The remedy was to try and give a wide enough variety of choices and opportunities for writing, reading, and talking so that everyone would have a fairly

good chance of showing his best talents. It is not just in English that it makes no sense to figure students' grades by taking an average of all their daily or weekly work. It makes no sense in any subject. It is not grading alone that is stupid, but the whole idea of trying to have a class move along on a schedule, like a train. Children do not learn things at the same time, or equally easily and quickly.

Grades

If you feel you must assign grades due to regulations or other influences—for instance, at times unschooled children ask for grades—here is some advice. John Holt advised teachers in school to "grade as little and as lightly as possible." This is a tactical idea so the students won't automatically feel that grades are the focus and purpose of learning. However, even if your local education authority (LEA) insists that you assign grades as school does, you still have options. First, confirm that the law or regulation cited by the LEA is accurately interpreted. Often, school officials assume what is needed in their school is also what is required in home schools, and this is often not true. Homeschooling often has different reporting options and you should be aware of them for your own use.

I recommend reading Kathy Ceceri's article about evaluating a child's progress in home school [http://homeschooling.about.com/od/records/fl/Do-I-Have-to-Give-Grades.htm]. Here is her information about calculating grades if you must give them.

You can choose to give your child grades just like the schools do. Giving your child grades can also look better on college and scholarship applications, even if they are so-called "mommy grades." Some of the grading methods homeschoolers use include:

Letter Grades: The standard A–F grading system, with "A" or "A+" being the high end of the scale, and "F" indicating failing. Letter grades sound impressive, but they can be given subjectively.

Number Grades: These are usually expressed as a percentage, with 100% being a perfect score and anything over some number, usually 65%, considered a passing grade. Number grades are typically based upon the percentage of correct answers (or on points earned for correct work) on homework, tests, and assignments.

Grade Point Average: The GPA is derived by taking the average of the number grades (on a scale of 1 to 4) for each class, multiplied by the number of credits that class is worth. So a 3.5 (roughly a B+) in a four-credit science class will bring the GPA up more than the same grade in a three-credit math class.

Pass/Fail (or Satisfactory/Unsatisfactory): Some schools use this grading system in the early years. Students are considered to have passed as long as they have achieved the minimum goals for the class. If you would rather not give your child grades but your state or district requires it, this could be a good compromise.

Alternatives to Grades

In states that require homeschoolers to provide a form of evaluation during, or at the end of, the school year, homeschoolers can often choose from the following evaluation methods.

Portfolios and other descriptive measures of learning are well suited for families who want to get away from grades and gold stars, particularly if they aren't following a conventional school curriculum.

Standardized Testing

This can be provided by the school, or, in some cases, you can negotiate to use a third party, such as a guidance counselor, teacher, or mutually agreed upon proctor, to administer the test in your home. If you feel the school's choice of test is biased against your homeschooling methods and philosophy, you can ask to administer a different test more to your liking. Before doing this, it is wise to consider how and what you will be teaching your children; if you are following a school curriculum and periodically giving your children tests, then they are probably ready to take these standardized tests. If you have created an individualized study plan for your child, and you do not use standardized testing during your homeschooling year, but your school is forcing standardized tests on you (and you've checked to be sure there are no other options you can use), then it is wise to do as they do in school: get a hold of previous editions of the test, spend some time teaching the subject matter that you see is on the test (that is, teach to the test), and practice taking the test with your children.

Portfolio Assessments

This, combined with a yearly progress report, is how my family handled evaluations of our three children for our local district in MA (our girls are grown women now). A portfolio is an extension of the refrigerator magnet: a place where you save and date your children's work. The difference is you want to save a lot of this stuff and sift through it later to find significant pieces of achievement or indications of development for school officials, such as the two-page report on "The Real Pocahontas" our daughter Lauren (then nine) did, or problem solving, such as a series of math problems, with her self-corrections, that Alison (then six) did. We also save workbook pages (our children sometimes ask for workbook pages just to see if they can do the same stuff their schooled friends do!), lists of books we buy or check out from the library to read to them or that they read themselves, and brief journal notes about significant events, such as a trip to Plymouth Plantation when Lauren and a friend helped bake bread and make candles "the real way" by spending all day in one "Pilgrim's" house. Please note, the school never once asked to examine our portfolio for any of our girls; our annual progress report about their learning always proved to be sufficient.

Progress Reports

These can take the form of written narratives of your children's learning over a quarter, a half-year, or a year; the periodicity of these reports will depend on your state laws or regulations. Consider that if you write at least one sentence a day, or at least five sentences at the end of each week, about each child, by the end of the year you will have many pages of detailed information about what your children actually did, rather than just a letter or number for a year 's worth of work. There's no need to go overboard with listing accomplishments; one or two examples for each subject you want to describe should be enough.

Performance Assessments

This term refers to the evaluation of the culmination of a body of work. These are becoming more in vogue with some current education reforms. For example, a child could successfully build a working volcano to demonstrate mastery of certain science principles, or actually perform in a play or concert to demonstrate ability and understanding. Many real-life activities demonstrate thought, responsibility, planning, and subject mastery. For example, a child might, for the ultimate purpose of setting up an aquarium, determine how much money he has, budget it properly, and choose the right fish and equipment. Though it may sound like a homeschooling story, this particular example is taken from literature by the Wisconsin Department of Education about how it plans to evaluate students as part of its education reforms. Assessments can also take the form of interviews with other types of educators (child psychologists, school counselors, etc.); written reports from people other than relatives and parents who work with your child; and videotapes, audio tapes, and newspaper clippings of activities your children do that prove they can use the skills and knowledge they have learned.

Teach to Mastery

Mastery Learning has been around education circles since the 1960s and was pioneered by Benjamin S. Bloom [http://eric.ed.gov/?id=ED457185]. The goal isn't to get high grades with this process; instead, it provides evidence that the student understands the subject by their mastery of tasks and their ability to articulate the subject matter. Individualized instruction is provided as needed to each student rather than classroom lectures.

PROTECT UNSCHOOLING FROM INTRUSIVE EDUCATION PRACTICES

When one's home life is intimately entwined with one's education, it can feel that school concerns about grade levels or textbook choices are unwelcome intrusions into one's family. Here are two stories about observing and reporting unschooling without interfering with your children's learning or judging them as school does. (Reprinted from *Growing Without Schooling* 78.)

Finding Things Out

Wendy Martyna of California sent us the "Home School Report" she'd written at the end of the year. Some excerpts:

We often play what we call "The Question Game," where one of us poses a question (usually of central philosophical importance) that the others each get to answer in any way they like. Examples: "What is truth?" "Why do people not know that the Earth is alive, and hurt her?" "What is times?" The other day, 7-year old Miles' question was, "What is smart?" and our answers reflected a deep sense that knowledge is only part of smartness.

Bryn (10) said that some people think smart is knowing lots of things, like things you memorize or learn in school. We all agreed that smart is knowing how-to find out things, and knowing what you do not know, and being willing to not know.

I recently read parts of a book by Richard Saul Wurman, *Information Anxiety*, which assesses the overwhelming quality of the information we are confronted with daily, and defines information anxiety as the gap between what we know and what we think we should know. He says his father taught him not that he should know everything in the encyclopedia, but that he should show how to find it. When I observe Bryn's and Miles' learning process, I see no anxiety about what they do not know (except in the momentary frustration of trying to solve an immediate problem before them), and I see great skill in finding out what they need or want to know. I also see an intense commitment to learning, and an individual sense of timing that guides them.

Miles can spend an hour or more immersed in reading a Tintin adventure book, and not even hear us calling him. The next day, he may spend that same intense hour experimenting with a mylar dancing ribbon on a stick, watching and controlling the many patterns and motions it can make (and telling me about it as he does). Both of them follow their heart when it comes to learning—which may mean wanting to do a math workbook in the car on Sunday when we're driving somewhere. You never know what you can count on is that they are doing, most of the time, what they want to be doing, for their own reasons, and finding meaning—a sense of internal purpose—in doing it.

. . . Both the children like to have assessments when they ask for them or when I offer them and they agree. They do not resist structure or evaluation, but rather are free to enjoy its pleasures, because it comes purely, without strings. When I made up a worksheet for them—one on Tintin books, one on Madeline L'Engle—they couldn't wait till they were printed off the computer to start on them.

. . . When we are watering the garden, weeding the strawberries, bemoaning the gophers' holes, studying the rebirth and unfolding of a calla lily, we are often taken afield (or "agarden") into other discussions or experiments. And we end up learning quite a bit, learning in a way that might take us back into a book, or a drawing. But that was not the point, or even the purpose. The point was to water the garden, or weed the strawberries. The learning, ultimately, is not extractable from the unfolding of the experience, so that to tell about it is different than it was. But to tell about it in these other ways also carries a truth—it is a truth that belongs to reflection afterwards (as when one, at 38, comes to understand in quite a different way what one was doing at 19). This is why we don't hear ourselves saying, "well, now we are having a lesson in physics" with that "let's turn to chapter" tone of voice, but rather find ourselves looking well into the learning itself, as it emerges out of the truth of the moment.

Looking back and reflecting on it the lesson may well have much beyond physics in it—what might be called literature, and philosophy, and biology, and much more. That doesn't mean that the children—or Bill or I—wouldn't hear ourselves saying (in wonder, sometimes, or just as a comment on the situation), "Well, here we are talking about geography now!" But it wouldn't be that sneaky kind of creeping up and pouncing on "the teachable moment," still assuming that learning needs to take a specified form and be caught in the act before it can be said to have occurred. In fact, the phrase 'the teachable moment' seems to imply that some moments are not teachable or worse, that teaching is something that needs to be added to the moment, rather than discovered within it. . . .

Retention. Comprehension. These things become natural byproducts of the kind of learning they experience. I was reading a book aloud to both of them, and Miles had read to himself another of the books in that series. I had wondered if that book was too difficult for him to read, but he sat and read it right through. I wondered if he had retained it, but I found out without asking or testing. As I read the other book aloud, he continually told us all that had happened to each of those characters in the other book, and the opinion on what had happened. And Bryn recounts plots in compelling ways, when she is done with or even midway through her books. And Miles is the master of *The Adventures of Tintin* detail—if we play "21 Questions" about a Tintin fact Miles is the acknowledged master of us all.

Tintin reminds me of something that's also fundamentally important to our homeschooling process. That is the role that Bill and I play, as teachers and learners and parents and companions. A mix of roles that alter according to mood and context, but that reduces down to a deep sense we both have that we are privileged to all be on this journey together. When I found myself wondering what Miles was seeing in these many Tintin books, what was absorbing him so, and found also that I was worried about the racial stereotypes in the books and the occasional use of violence, I did some research. Of course, we talked about the racial stereotypes and that became a chance to recognize them when they occur, especially in subtle form, and in historical context. But there was more I wanted to know, that he was not interested in explaining (why he liked them was not interesting to him at the time, only that he liked them). In the library reference room I looked up the author and xeroxed pages of biographical information, and then found about twenty pages of critical essays concerning Tintin in the *Book Review Index*. In reading these, I learned a lot, and what I learned deepened my understanding of the mythic quality of the Tintin adventure, and helped to answer many questions, to stimulate my reflections, not Miles'. It was to satisfy my need to know, not his. Because we try to keep that view in mind—that it is our questions and our learning that are also involved in homeschooling, we help ourselves avoid the trap of feeling self-sacrificing, given the enormous commitment required. We try to keep the sense of privilege alive. It is the same as with being parents—cultivating not a sense that we are "doing all this for you," or even the opposite, that they are doing it all for us, that we are only awed witnesses of the magic that children offer. It is, rather, something integrated, something inseparable.

———————

From a later letter Wendy wrote us:

You asked me to tell you exactly what the 'Home School Report' was written for. Our Independent Home Study Program is affiliated with the Loma Prieta School District. They require that we submit monthly or quarterly reports, and these need to include the things the children have been doing or working on in science, math, language, etc. I have always listed events and activities in a long list under each category (always struggling to reconstruct what I should have kept more careful track of, and then felt so much was missing from that kind of report). So, last June, I was working with some writing I was doing about our lives, and decided to submit that along with the lists. This report, then, was submitted as an official report, and occurred in response to that assignment. But it went beyond the bounds of the assignment and was truly done for me.

Not On Display

From a longer paper that Jutta Mason sent us:

Inside our house, activities are not noted down, nor are they marked. If one of the children does a puzzle or reads a book there are no congratulations or prizes; if someone makes a mistake there may be regret, but without public humiliation. The children look out at the world without a sense of being on display. As I write this, on a Friday morning. I'm sitting in front of the fireplace beside my daughter, who is reading a novel. Her brothers are at the table, playing chess. Outside the window the dog is gnawing at a stick. We're at a cottage, in the woods. If we were at home, I might be typing into the computer, and the kids might be walking over to the grocery store to do the weekly shopping (the store delivers). Or my younger one might be roaring around the back lane with his friends, with me making supper in the kitchen, *The Magic Flute* on the tape deck, the older children mimicking the opera singers for my amusement! We pass in and out of one another's occupations and nobody is noting down the hours of music appreciation, physical fitness, literary studies, grocery math, or geography. My younger son comes to me with his hands full of matchboxes, to tell me that if all the boxes are full, he will have 210 matches. He shows me, grinning, how he figured this out without counting each one separately. Ever since he was quite small he's always looked out for numbers and the ordering of things. This doesn't mean he'll one day be a mathematician, nor even that he'll be recognized as "good at math," it means nothing except what it is: his pleasure at figuring out the number 210. In the same way, our comings together in the household at various times of the day means nothing more than just the pleasure (or, at other times, the difficulty) of each other's company. The spaces inside our household are personal, not public, and unmonitored for productivity. But all of us can do things there that interest us very much. This is at our best, and after some struggle. As a graduate of years of compulsory schooling, I am used to looking outside myself for professional sanction and approval of what I do. I used to monitor my children as though there were an invisible school officials looking over my shoulder. The children's comments about numbers or stars or insects would often be channeled into further questions about mathematics or astronomy or zoology. This slowed down when I noticed the children were avoiding me. My daughter didn't mention numbers for over a month when I once used a question she asked me as an opportunity to show her the ministry guidelines on primary grade mathematics. I took her reaction as a caution rather than a challenge.

School officials came to our house to check our children's math proficiency. The kids were mystified by the strange plastic money the officials brought, and could hardly add six and six (after months of the most complex allowance transactions). I took this as another caution. My daughter resisted even my feeble attempts to get her to read, until she was 9. Then she began to read, not "Dick and Jane" books, but her favorite novels. Now she reads faster than her father, who reads for a living. My next child, in the meantime, sat in his room and figured out how to read by himself, before I really noticed. I'm not sure what his method was. Here was a third caution to me. In our family, learning to read turned out to be like learning to walk and to talk—everyone eventually does it. As my instructing diminished, our conversations expanded. The conversations flourished the more they were unplanned. An engaging topic could strike at any time: while walking the dog, driving somewhere, winding down for bed, having lunch, digging in the garden, opening the mail, having an argument. As the years move on, I am sometimes astonished at the privilege I have of seeing how these three young ones unfold and take in the world around them. They learn next to me but only sometimes, at their own choosing, because of me. And they learn plenty.

Some people may wonder how we can satisfy the homeschooling regulations without noting down our children's activities and evaluating them. In Ontario the regulations are still pleasantly vague. The ministry of education is required to make sure that "satisfactory education" is being provided for each child, but "satisfactory" is not defined. So the school superintendents of each area have to interpret this themselves. They are very busy people, as are the consultants they send out to visit homeschooling families. I have tried to take advantage of this business by preempting any school officials to structure our activities. Twice a year I send a fat essay to the school officials, a rambling tale about what the kids have been up to in the previous six months. They didn't ask me to do this—I decided on this routine myself. I divide up my narrative anyway I like. At the beginning I sorted our activities by school subject category; later on I sorted more by my

47

own inclinations. Writing these reports has been fun for me because I have chosen to be fairly frank and also because I get to go on at length about our adventures. It's not often that you have a captive audience to talk to about your kids. Because each of these documents have been at least ten pages long, I imagine they give a pleasant bulk to the school's files on the children, hopefully satisfying the bureaucratic requirement for well-filled files. I don't have the impression that the school officials read what I write very carefully; it's the form, not the content that counts. Wherever the kids could be seen as noticeably "behind" standardized school learning schedules, such as in their late reading, the absence of formal math learning, and their lack of French, I try to explain this as a careful decision by David and me. Being on the offensive rather than the defensive seems helpful here. When the absence of reading, math, or French instruction are presented as an intentional part of what the school officials can imagine as our "curriculum" (a word that I avoid like the plague), they can file us under the category of eccentric educational philosophy, rather than child neglect. So far this has worked out for us: we have been left in peace. There's no insurance that it will continue to work, but I have chosen to appreciate the grace of the present rather than to anticipation the troubles of the future.

――――――

[Susannah Sheffer, the editor of *Growing Without Schooling,* added:] Readers often ask us how they can claim to be teaching reading, and thereby satisfying that part of their state's homeschooling regulations, if their child isn't reading at all. We usually give just the advice that Jutta gives: you want, above all, to avoid giving the impression that you haven't noticed that your child isn't reading (or whatever the subject may be), don't think it's important, etc. That's just too much for school officials to understand or accept, even if it may be true. You don't want to seem to be neglecting your child, as Jutta says. But if you can make it clear that your child's late reading (or, at any rate, your belief that it's OK if children read at later ages) is an integral part of your educational beliefs, supported by the following studies, sources, and so on, that makes a difference. If this isn't true—that is, if you really do wish your child were reading—you can still protect him or her from further pressure by making clear what you plan to do about reading for the following year: "For Johnny's fifth grade year, we will be reading aloud from the following books, visiting the library regularly, discussing the daily newspaper . . . " etc. The point is, you can make it clear that you are giving reading some time and attention without making any promises about exactly when your child will be reading on his own.

EDUCATIONESE

In the early days of homeschooling, when it was not a widely known practice, we at HoltGWS recommended using some education jargon in your reports so the school official reading it would have a hook to grasp your meaning, or at least think that you are serious about education by sharing their vocabulary. For instance, if your child read a book over the course of a day, you can write that he or she "engaged in uninterrupted silent sustained reading (USSR) for x number of hours." Since the 1980s, I've collected and read lots of educationese and here are some resources for you to ponder and use as you need, as well as some commonly used phrases by schools that are deciphered for you.

Criterion-referenced assessment. How your children scored on a test of the material they were supposed to learn.

Dynamic assessment. "Dynamic assessment . . . is . . . an effort to find the characteristics, especially the potential for effective learning, of individuals without reference to the performance of others."— *Dynamic Assessment in Practice: Clinical and Educational Applications.*
[http://assets.cambridge.org/052184/9357/excerpt/0521849357_excerpt.htm]

51

ELO—Embedded learning opportunities. Example: Shopping and making correct change for purchases.

Feedback versus Evaluation. Evaluation is typically a grade or a short comment on a report card. Feedback is detailed information about what a student actually did and what they might do to improve.

Learner-initiated activity. Example: A child wants to create a song, learn to ride a bike, or understand how to do Sudoko puzzles and does so.

Norm-referenced assessment. How your children scored as compared to other children.

Project learning. Example: Building a scale model of the U.S.S. Constitution is a project that also encompasses history, science, math, and so on. This one project can overlap many subject areas and usually produces a final product at completion, such as a science fair project.

Self-test/self-assessment. Example: A child chooses to see if they can read a Harry Potter book on their own, play or sing a song, and so on, and then determines how well he or she did.

Self-correction. Example: A child notices she made an arithmetic mistake or speaking error and corrects herself.

Uninterrupted silent sustained reading (USSR). If you have a child who likes to read, this is a great phrase to use. In school, it often refers to recreational (that is, self-chosen) reading, which indicates a learner-initiated activity and possibly self-correction and self-assessment, too.

Unit Studies. This refers to covering many different subjects that relate to one broad topic. Example: An interest in automobiles may lead to reading about the history of cars, drawing cars, building models of cars, creating types of engines to propel homemade cars (rubber bands, batteries, etc.), visiting a car dealer or manufacturer, helping to tune up a car engine, and so on. Each one of these units of study strengthens one's overall knowledge about automobiles.

Edu-Speak [http://ulfaq.home.comcast.net/~ulfaq/eduspeak.html]

I discovered this online dictionary about educationese and don't know whether to laugh or cry when I refer to it. Edu-Speak list member, professor Lonnie Turbee, notes why this language exists:

One of the reasons educrats use language like this is because, whether they're conscious of it or not, it gives them power over us mere "lay" parents. It has actually worked to intimidate *me*! I never became a public school teacher (I've always taught at the university level), so I never had a professional reason to "cognitively interact" with such drivel, although I've read plenty of the nonsense that shows up in professional journal articles—I may have written some of it myself. It's saddening to think of all the parents who are valiantly struggling to do their best by their kids *inside the school system* who are faced with educrats who use this kind of power play to keep everyone, kids and parents, under control.

Here are some more resources about how homeschoolers translate their daily activities into educationese for school reporting purposes.

1. Anne Zeise has some examples online [http://a2zhomeschool.com/homeschool/about/glossary/educationese-homeschool-reports/]. For instance, Anne notes that Arts and Crafts in

relation to any subject can be turned into educationese by stating, "Manipulative construction relating to _____ (name of subject)."

2. Cafi Cohen, in her book *Homeschooling: The Teen Years*, created a chart of educationese equivalents. For instance:

Reading the Daily Paper = Current Events, Social Studies
Playing Monopoly = Math
Genealogy = History, Language Arts
Cooking = Math, Science
Tae Kwan Do = Physical Education
Talking with Grandpa about His Life = History
Photography = Science, Art[3]

However, I've stopped using this language unless forced to do so since I feel it feeds the notion that for something to be important it must have a complex label approved and used by school (see Appendix 3).

---

[3] Cohen, Cafi. 2000. *Homeschooling the Teen Years*. Prima: Roseville, CA, 30.

ONLINE EXAMPLES OF UNSCHOOLING REPORTS ACCEPTED BY SCHOOLS

My Unschoolers' End-of-the-Year Reports.

An Australian unschooler shares her reports. http://www.storiesofanunschoolingfamily.com/2012/12/my-unschoolers-end-of-year-reports.html

Learning Logs by Ivy Rutledge.

A good essay about how the author's family brainstorms their learning efforts together.

http://homeedmag.com/HEM/231/learninglogs.php

Two sample progress reports, as well as much good information about writing your homeschooling plan and report, are provided by Advocates for Home Education in Massachusetts (www.ahem.info).

> Report A [http://www.ahem.info/ProgressReportA.html] is extremely brief and to the point.
>
> Report B [http://www.ahem.info/ProgressReportB.html] is more detailed. You can use these as models to build your own report.

Undogmatic Unschoolers: Learning and Progress Reports. Based in the Canadian province of Alberta, this family shares their learning plans and progress reports for their two children over a period of seven years. I like how this family calls attention to the fact that their plans "get skimpier and skimpier with each year . . . and the progress reports less and less aligned to school subjects" as their children learn, grow and mature.

https://undogmaticunschoolers.wordpress.com/unschooling-in-calgary/learning-plans-progress-reports/

APPENDIX 1

Research That Supports Unschooling/Self-Directed Learning

Aiken, Wilford M. 1942. *The Story of the Eight-Year Study*. Harper & Brothers: New York. A high-quality, long-term study of the effects that attending an alternative high school had upon college success. Shows there are many paths for college success besides high grades from a college preparatory school.

Gray, Peter. 2013. *Free to Learn: Why Unleashing the Instinct to Play Will Make Our Children Happier, More Self-Reliant, and Better Students for Life*. Basic Books: New York. See pp. 93–100 regarding educational attainment for self-directed learners.

Hannam, Derry. 2001. *A Pilot Study to Evaluate the Impact of the Student Participation Aspects of The Citizenship Order on Standards of Education in Secondary Schools*. Strongly supports letting students be involved in planning their learning and running their school.
http://alternativestoschool.com/pdfs/The%20Hannam%20Report.pdf.

The Journal of Unschooling and Alternative Learning [http://jual.nipissingu.ca/] published by the Schulich School of

Education, Graduate Studies, Nipissing University, Ontario, Canada.

Superintendent Louis Benezet's Math Experiment [http://www.inference.phy.cam.ac.uk/sanjoy/benezet/]. Benezet abolished math studies from the seventh grade down and had the children read, recite, and reason instead. When they learned math, they did very well.

Thomas, Alan and Harriet Pattison. 2007. *How Children Learn at Home*. London: Continuum Books.

Thomas, Alan. 2005. *Educating Children at Home*. London: Continuum. Of particular note is Dr. Thomas' research on older readers and homeschooling. He finds no special learning issues among children who learn to read at older ages.

Unschooling and Self-Directed Learning Research
https://www.johnholtgws.com
http://www.alternativestoschool.com

General Research About Homeschooling
http://icher.org/ The International Center for Home Education Research
http://www.nheri.org/ National Home Education Research Institute

APPENDIX 2

John Holt prepared the following statement to accompany his appearance on a panel discussion before the Committee on Education of the Massachusetts State Legislature in October 1981. We see the statement as possibly a very useful tool for many homeschooling families, and hope that many people will include these points in their proposals, legal briefs, letters to authorities, and so on.

Following the suggestions of several helpful lawyers, we have revised some of the wording to make the arguments more persuasive in a court of law. Please note that while these arguments are all drawn from court rulings, they have not yet been tested in court as a single brief, in the form we give them here. They are of course not guaranteed to be foolproof, but we think they would be upheld in many courts. One attorney has already told us that a judge to whom he showed them found them convincing. More to the point, we think they will be strong enough to persuade many school systems not to try to take families to court, or legislators not to try to pass anti-homeschooling laws.

We also want to emphasize that we do not feel that homeschooling families should rush into the court as soon as they meet (if they do) some opposition from their local schools. For many reasons, the best policy for these families is to stay out of court if they can, for as long as they can. That they have tried to do so will be seen by most courts as a strong point in their favor, if the schools unwisely insist on pushing matters that far.

If you do circulate and/or use this statement, we would like to hear what sort of responses and results you get.

SUMMARY

1. The U.S. Constitution, under the First, Ninth, and Fourteenth Amendments, protects the rights of parents to get for their children the kind of education they want.
2. The Supreme Court, in *Pierce v. Society of Sisters* (1925) and *Farrington v. Tokushige* (1927), in upholding this right, said that the states could not, either through laws or regulations, impose a uniform system of education on all children.
3. Where the Supreme Court has upheld that the states have the legal power, under the Constitution, to regulate the education of children, it has done so on this ground alone, that the people have a right to protect themselves against the danger that uneducated children might grow up so ignorant as to be unemployable and a burden to the state.
4. The states have no Constitutional mandate to spread good ideas or stamp out bad ones, or to provide children with some kind of social life, or to carry out any other purposes

except the very limited one stated in #3 above.

5. The Constitutional right of parents to control the education of children is much broader than the Constitutionally permissible power of the states to control that education.

6. The states have the legal power to assure themselves that homeschooling parents are indeed doing something to educate their children, and that what the parents are doing is not manifestly harmful. They will in fact be far more able to do this if they cooperate with and support homeschooling families, rather than oppose them.

7. Since any laws making homeschooling difficult or impossible will be un-Constitutional and will be struck down by the courts, the legislature would do well not to pass such laws. It might even be helpful to make clear, by resolution or by amendment to the existing education statutes, that the intent of the compulsory education laws is not to empower the state or the several school districts to impose a uniform system of education on all parents.

STATEMENT

The educational alternative I wish to present here is what I will call homeschooling or home-based education, in which parents, instead of having their school-aged children in formal schools during school hours, teach them at home and in the world around the home, using the school as a resource only if and when they wish to.

Please understand first of all that this is not a new idea. The new idea is that children (or people of any age) can only learn in special learning places where nothing but learning happens. Even a century and a half ago, many American children rarely if ever attended a formal school and learned most of what they knew outside schools. At the turn of the century only six percent of our population even finished high school. And even in this century there have been many Americans, often successful and distinguished, who as children were rarely in a school setting. What we are talking about here is not a new idea but a rebirth of an old one.

In this statement I do not want to discuss the merits of this activity—I do this at length in my recent book *Teach Your Own*—but rather point out that the right of parents to teach their own children is very strongly supported by the Constitution and the courts, and that the power of the states to control this activity has been held to be a very narrow and limited one.

The Constitution itself is, of course, altogether silent on the matter of education. When it was written, most people did in fact educate their own children, with little outside help or interference. The framers of the Constitution would have found it hard to imagine either our present rigid and punitive compulsory education laws or our enormous centrally directed educational establishment.

They said nothing about education in the Constitution because they assumed that free American citizens could be trusted to go on educating their children as, with few exceptions, they had in the past.

But later on one group of Americans, for the most part native-born, wealthy, and politically powerful, began to fear that there were more and more people in the country, notably immigrants, who for one reason or another could not be trusted to educate their own children. It was because of this fear that they created our present institutions of compulsory schooling.

Because the Constitution is silent about the right of parents to educate their children does not mean that the framers felt they had no such right. We consider many rights to be Constitutionally protected that are not specifically mentioned, among these the right to choose our work and our homes, to travel, to marry whom we like, and so on. In the case of *Perchemlides v. Frizzle*, Massachusetts Superior Court Judge John Greaney ruled that the right of parents to control the education of their children must be considered as one of these Constitutionally protected rights. He located this right not only in the First and Fourteenth Amendments, as had frequently been held in other rulings, but also in the Ninth Amendment, which guarantees to citizens the right to control their private lives.

This right of parents to control the education of their children has over the years been upheld by many federal and state court rulings. The most important of these, the Constitutional bedrock on which homeschooling stands, are *Pierce vs. Society of Sisters* (1925) and *Farrington vs. Tokushige* (1927).

In *Pierce* the U.S. Supreme Court struck down an Oregon statute abolishing all private schools. It is worth noting that the Oregon legislature passed such a law for the very reason even now put forward by school authorities as an argument against homeschooling, namely, that unless all children were compelled to attend uniform state schools, the parents of many of them might be able to pass on to them various kinds of bad and dangerous ideas. Several schools, Catholic and secular, took the matter to the U. S. Supreme Court The Court ruled that while the states were Constitutionally permitted (on very narrow grounds, of which more later) to compel and regulate the education of children, they could not say that all children had to be educated in the same places or in the same way, but that parents had a right to get for their children an education in harmony with their own principles and beliefs. In effect, the Court said that the state could not run an educational monopoly, a fact not understood by too many educators even today.

In *Farrington* the Court reaffirmed and strengthened this position. At issue here was a set of regulations which the then territory of Hawaii was seeking to impose on all private schools, most notably a system of Japanese language private schools. These schools took the regulations to court, saying that they were so detailed and restrictive that their effect would be to destroy the unique identity of the Japanese language schools and to force them instead to become identical to the public schools. The Supreme Court struck down the regulations, saying, in effect, that the states could not do through regulations what it had already said they could not do through laws, i.e., impose an essentially uniform system of education on all citizens.

In Kentucky, two years or so ago, the State Board of Education tried to close down a number of private religious schools on the grounds that they were not following the state prescribed curriculum and that their teachers were not certified. The private schools, very ably defended in this case by William Ball of Harrisburg, PA, challenged the state to show that its regulations had produced better results in its own schools, and that certified teachers could teach better than uncertified. In his decision upholding the private schools, District Judge Henry Meigs said, "Expert testimony in this case certainly established that there is not the slightest connection between teacher certification and enhanced educational quality in State schools, nor is there generally any such requirement in private schools." The decision was upheld by the State Supreme Court and left to stand by the U.S. Supreme Court

Since then, courts in three other states have challenged the state to show evidence for the superiority of certified teachers, with the same result—the states could not, for in fact no such evidence exists. It is indeed easily verifiable that the most notable, selective, and successful of the nation's private colleges and secondary schools have on their faculties very few people with teacher's certificates or training in education.

In many other states, including Illinois, Massachusetts, New Jersey, and Indiana, courts have ruled that the rights established in *Pierce* and *Farrington* extend to parents who wish to teach their own children. It is clear, then, that the activity of homeschooling rests on very solid Constitutional ground.

Against this right of parents to control their children's education must be balanced an opposing right, the right of the people in society to insure that all children are educated, and so to enact and enforce compulsory education laws. The Supreme Court has upheld this right many times, usually against claims of a religious nature. But it is important to understand that the Court has upheld this right on one ground and one only, namely, that under the police powers reserved to them, the states may protect society against the possibility that children may grow up so ignorant that they will be a burden to the society, unemployable, and unable to carry out the minimum duties of citizenship. Anything the states may wish to do in their schools, if contested on Constitutional grounds, must be measured against this standard.

In other words, just because the Court has upheld compulsory education as being permitted under the Constitution, it does not follow that the state schools have a Constitutional mandate for anything and everything they may happen to want to do. Except for things specifically illegal, they may do whatever they want—provided that nobody objects. It is only when parents object that the Constitutional power of the schools to do what they are doing comes into question.

Thus, most people are more or less content to have the schools teach, as final and permanent truths, the latest theories of scientists, physical or social. But when some parents say, as more and more now say, "We don't want our children to be told that this or that scientific theory is true, or even that truth can only come out of scientific laboratories," then we have to ask whether the courts have given the state schools a Constitutional mandate to teach such "truths." The answer is that they have not—unless they can show that children who do not believe these school-proclaimed "truths" are likely to become a burden to the state. In short, the schools have no Constitutional mandate to declare that some ideas are good and others bad.

Let us face squarely this question in its most difficult form. Suppose some parents were teaching their children that all people of a certain skin color or religion or national origin or political persuasion were so evil that the children had a moral duty to kill them on sight. Would the state not then be able to say that it had the legal power to prevent the parents from teaching those beliefs? In such a case, the courts could be expected to apply the rule of "clear and present danger." In other words, the state, in order to step in legally, would have to show that there was an immediate danger that the children would put those ideas into action.

After all, many established religions teach their believers that all non-believers are enemies. Many Christian sects teach that non-Christians, or even Christians of other sects, are heretics, evil, damned, agents of Satan, etc. Black Muslims were for a while and may still be teaching, as part of their religion, that all white people are devils. Yet nowhere have the courts denied such people and such religious institutions the right to spread such beliefs.

Even if they did hold that in some particular case there was a clear and present danger that the children would commit the crimes their parents were telling them to commit, the courts would not be so foolish as to say that the remedy for this was to send the children to school, so that they could there be taught correct ideas. If the danger was truly clear and present—remember Justice Holmes' example of a man shouting "Fire!" in a crowded theatre—the only sensible remedy for the state would be to remove the children from the custody of the parents altogether. But no parents, even members of the Nazi party or Ku Klux Klan, have ever been deprived of the custody of their children for this reason.

It seems clear, then, that we cannot say that because under some special circumstances the teaching of certain bad ideas to certain children might present a clear and immediate danger to the state, the schools must therefore be considered to have a general Constitutional mandate to stamp out bad ideas and spread good ones. Who would have the power to decide which ideas were good and which bad? How would we elect or appoint our Commissar of Correct thought? The notion is as abhorrent as it is absurd. It follows, then, that the schools cannot Constitutionally prohibit parents from teaching their own children on the grounds that they might be teaching some bad ideas or not teaching some good ones—unless, as I have said before, they could show that because of having or not having these ideas children would grow up unemployable and a burden to the state.

By the same token, most people are willing to accept the "social life" of the schools, on the grounds that it is some kind of preparation for "Real Life," by which they almost always mean something bad, that cannot be changed but must only be endured. (A strange way for a free people to talk!) As long as no one complains, no Constitutional issue is raised. But when some parents say, as more and more do, "We don't approve of this social life and the values it teaches, and we don't want this social life for our children," then we must ask, as before, do the schools have a Constitutional mandate to provide some kind of approved social life for children? The answer is, they do not. Can the schools show convincing evidence, or any at all, that unless children have this school-type social life they are likely to become a burden to the state? They can not. Indeed, a strong case could be made that the social life of many schools tends to destroy rather than create positive and healthy attitudes toward work. (One brief example would be the prevalence of cheating, even in our supposedly "best" schools.)

It was just for such reason that Massachusetts Superior Court Judge Greaney, in *Perchemlides v. Frizzle*, ruled that the local school district could not use the absence of a school-like social life as a reason for disapproving of a family's home education program.

Many parents seem willing to accept, perhaps because they believe in it, perhaps because they can't imagine anything else, a method of education based on the assumption that children will not learn anything important unless made to, and that the best way to make them is to give them long lists of disconnected facts to memorize and repeat on demand. But other people, myself among them, believe very strongly (as I wrote many years ago in *How Children Fail*) that these conventional methods of education do not help learning but instead prevent it, and indeed destroy most of children's desire and ability to learn. Many parents say, "Until they went to school, our children were curious, eager, confident, resourceful, independent, skillful learners. Now we see them becoming every day more and more bored, uncurious, unmotivated, dependent, timid, self-despising, too terrified of failure to be willing any more to try the new or explore the unknown. Why must we put up with methods of education that are destroying the intelligence and character of our children?"

There is no Constitutional reason why they should. In fact,

the state schools cannot show that anything they do produces better results than other methods—not their choice of what subjects to teach, or the ages at which they teach them, or their ways of teaching them, or their ways of teaching, testing, evaluating, grouping, and scheduling, or their textbooks and other materials. Often, as in Kentucky, they cannot even show that their results are as good. There are many schools all over the country whose curricula and methods are completely different from the state schools, like Montessori schools, or Waldorf (Steiner) schools, where children are not formally instructed in reading until the age of 10, that have shown outstanding results. Still other schools achieve equally successful results in spite of having very little formal curriculum or none at all.

But even if the state schools could show that their curricula, etc. did in fact produce substantially better results, they still would not have the power under the Constitution to impose these on all parents. For what the Supreme Court in *Pierce* and *Farrington* said to the states was not that they could impose a uniform system of education on all parents, provided only that they show that it produced better results. It said that they could not impose a uniform system *at all*. The schools, in other words, can not tell parents how they must educate their children unless they can show that without such restrictions some children might become a burden on the state.

Let me sum up what I have said here. The courts have held

that parents have a Constitutional right to exercise control over the education of children, and that schools have the power also to exercise control over the education of children. But the rights of the parents are very broad, the power of the schools very narrow. Some might argue that the power of the state and the schools, as defined here, are so narrow as to be equal to no power at all, but that is not the case. The state does not have power under the Constitution to tell parents how to educate their children, but it does have the power to assure itself that they are in fact doing something, and that what they are doing is not manifestly harmful. Thus the state would be altogether justified in being very skeptical and critical of the educational proposals of parents who were alcoholics or heavy drug users, or in constant trouble with the law, or whom it knew, or had strong reason to suspect, were already physically neglecting or abusing their children.

How then might, and should, the state exercise its power in the matter of homeschooling? As good fortune would have it, what the state has a Constitutional power to do is the very thing that it would be wisest to do anyway, which is to say to parents who wish to educate their children, as some school districts are already saying, "Tell us what you want to do in educating your children, and why you want to do it, and how you plan to assess it; send us a report once a year or so about what your children are doing and learning, with perhaps some samples of their work in various fields (the so-called 'portfolio method' of evaluation); don't hesitate to ask us for advice or help; and above all, feel free to use our schools and their many resources whenever you wish."

The portfolio method mentioned above was part of the agreement that was finally worked out, with the assistance of Dr. Mario Fantini, Dean of the School of Education at the University of Massachusetts, between the Perchemlides family and the Amherst School District. Several school districts in the state have said to homeschooling families that their children are welcome to use the school when and as they wish, i.e., to use the library, take a special course, sing in a chorus, play a sport, go on a field trip, or whatever. Clearly a school system that has declared itself a friend and supporter of a homeschooling family is much more likely to know what they are really doing, and to be in a position to help them, than a school that has told a homeschooling family that they can't teach their own children at all or can only do so if they use methods identical to the school's.

There is, after all, an inherent conflict of interest and a possibility for injustice when we ask state schools to evaluate the merits of a family's homeschooling plan. It is a little like telling people they can own any kind of car they want, as long as they have the approval of the local General Motors dealer. Judges must disqualify themselves in cases where they have a personal and/or material interest. Yet the state schools, with their declining budgets, can hardly be disinterested evaluators of family education plans; many a school superintendent has flatly told a family that he would not let them teach their children at home because of the state aid he would lose. (Though it is not clear why schools should not be able to collect state aid for children they are helping to learn at home, as they would if these children were being tutored at home only because they were ill.) People asked to assess homeschooling plans should, at the very least, be disinterested, and should not disapprove of homeschooling on principle.

It is possible that we may see in Massachusetts, as we have in other states, organized attempts to push through laws which would seriously limit or destroy altogether the right of parents to teach their own children. The claim is made that such laws are needed to "clarify" the existing education laws, or, as in Minnesota this very minute, to "protect the rights of educational consumers." These are smokescreens. These laws might better be called job protection laws, and their clear intent is to make it possible to prosecute families teaching their children at home or in small independent religious schools, and so to compel them to return their children to the state schools. Now a case could perhaps be made that all holders of teacher's certificates should be guaranteed teaching jobs throughout their working lifetime. But if legislatures wish to pursue this objective, they should do so directly, and not under the guise of maintaining educational standards or protecting educational consumers. If a campaign to pass such laws is mounted here in Massachusetts, the legislature would be wise to resist it. It will not solve the problems of the schools, but will only burden the courts with a wave of needless and fruitless litigation—fruitless, because such over-regulatory laws have already many times (beginning with *Farrington*) been struck down by the courts.

Indeed, it might help reduce the possibility of such needless litigation against parents if the legislature were to state, as an amendment to the compulsory education laws, that it was not the purpose of these laws to impose a uniform system of education on all children in the state or within any given school districts. Perhaps even a joint resolution to this effect by the Education Committees of the Legislature would achieve the same result. And, as I have said before, it would be helpful as well as fair if whatever regulations that govern the giving of state aid to local school districts could be amended so as to make it possible for the schools to collect this state aid for children who were learning at home with the school's cooperation and supervision.

APPENDIX 3

I gave a talk about educationese at the Cambridge Public Library in 2004 that I later summarized in this article.

Schools Are from Mars, Homeschoolers Are from Earth

I'm all for schools and homeschoolers figuring out how to peacefully co-exist—indeed, even cooperate—but sometimes I wonder if we're even talking about the same thing when we discuss children and learning. Judging by the language we use, I wonder if we're even on the same planet.

For instance, a mother tells me how her son read *Harry Potter and the Order of the Phoenix* twice on his own initiative. She allows him all day to read if he wishes. Most of us recognize what is going on here: a child is enjoying reading a book at home. But if you take that very same action and place it in a school, this no longer takes place. What happens in school is called "uninterrupted silent sustained reading."

If a homeschooler takes their child to a living history museum, such as Plymouth Plantation, they are likely to speak with different interpreters about their homes, histories, and daily lives. They may bake bread over an open hearth with a Pilgrim, or help an Indian make a canoe, or help a Pilgrim plot a garden during the course of their time. If the family has to report their learning to a school district, they will say they did a field trip, or undertook various activities and projects at Plymouth Plantation. But if you take this very same activity and place it in a school it becomes "an interdisciplinary unit study using learner-initiated activities."

I feel I am partly to blame for this decay of clarity, as I have counseled many homeschoolers to take their children's everyday activities and wrap them up in the jargon of school if they report their children's learning to school officials. Since learning at home is completely different from learning in school, sometimes school officials find it easier to approve or evaluate a homeschooling situation if there is academic jargon used by parents. Using such language can help establish parental seriousness and understanding in words the school will readily grasp. Not all states require you to report or evaluate your homeschooling progress, and there are some school officials who will accept common explanations of competence written in plain language.

For instance, by correctly tabulating a bowling score a child could prove their understanding of basic addition. I would tell my school district, "I know my daughter can add correctly because she keeps correct scores for our bowling league each week." A few schools would accept this evidence, or term it a "progress report," as stated. However for fussy school districts I would advise parents to write that their children are "modeling efficient addition strategies" by keeping correct bowling scores. Indeed, in some seminars I offer lists of "educationese" that can be adapted for use by homeschoolers in their attempts to speak the same language as their schools. For instance:

If your ten-year-old is spending days or weeks studying and performing magic tricks, reading books about designing illusions, and not much else that looks academic, you tell people and school officials they are doing "block learning" or "project learning" in language and theater arts.

If you don't want your child to take standardized tests because your curriculum is eclectic or totally learner-directed, you tell people and school officials that you will assess ("evaluate" is losing currency in current eduspeak) your children through "progress reports," or "portfolio evaluations" instead.

Some other examples of educationese are provided by Cafi Cohen in her book, *Homeschoolers' College Admissions Handbook:*[4]

Chess = critical thinking

Paintball = physical education

Visiting museums = history, science, and fine arts

Appliance repair = science

---

[4] Cohen, Cafi. 2000. *Homeschoolers' College Admissions Handbook*. Prima: Roseville, CA, 120—121).

Catalogs = consumer math

Fiction = contemporary literature

Nonfiction = science, history, language arts

As you can see, homeschoolers have tried to meet the schools halfway on this language issue. We are trying to be cooperative and provide schools with evidence that education is taking place for our children in words and concepts they should understand, but the schools have widened the gap again. *The Washington Post* ran the following article: "Talking the Edutalk: Jargon Becoming Prevalent in the Classroom" by Linda Perlstein (Sunday, January 18, 2004; Page A01). In it she notes the following developments in educationese:

6-year-olds don't compare books anymore—they make "text-to-text connections." Misbehaving students face not detention but the "alternative instruction room," or "reinforcement room," or "reflection room..."

And in Maryland, high schoolers write "extended constructed responses"—the essay, in a simpler time.

The most interesting quote for me in this good article came from a student:

> Robert Maeder, 17, a senior at Springbrook High School in Silver Spring, finds the terms demeaning—especially "learning cottage," instead of "classroom trailer," and "assessment" for test. "It's like renaming a prison 'The Happy Fun Place,' " Maeder said. "Tests should be called tests."

I don't think homeschoolers are deliberately polluting plainspoken discourse when they use eduspeak: they tend to use school jargon as self-defense for homeschooling, a kind of verbal judo to describe everyday life for children in academic language. Some school authorities justify their use of jargon by claiming these new terms are better descriptions of what children are doing, but I'll let the examples speak for themselves and let you be the judge of that claim.

As homeschooling continues to grow, I hope homeschoolers will resist the temptation of using jargon as the schools do, as a way to establish themselves as authorities over others. I'm also de-emphasizing the use of educationese by myself, because it seems to be yet another capitulation of everyday learning to the power of schooling. Rather than diminishing the power of these words and concepts by repeating them to the school to describe how our children grow without schooling, we may be inadvertently strengthening their grip on our ideas about learning. Homeschooling has grown by leaps and bounds over the years because it works, not because school officials, television shows, big business, or professors of education have blessed it with their approval and attention. Homeschooling has grown because people see it working for other families, and they can see how learning doesn't have to mean duplicating school at home. Homeschoolers are showing what active learning can be, and our numbers are increasing. Homeschoolers can also talk about what our kids are actually doing and learning in words people of all ages and backgrounds will readily understand, and this should help us all see that there are many other possibilities for helping children to learn and grow in our society than being educated in a school classroom. But somehow school people keep coming up with words that distance people who "learn outside the box," rather than include them.

I used to think that schools and homeschoolers had difficulty speaking to one another because, primarily, schools and homeschoolers are stuck in a battle about the boundaries of what is public and what is private in our lives. Now I realize it is much

simpler than that: schools are from Mars, homeschoolers are from Earth.

Made in the USA
Las Vegas, NV
04 December 2021

36075803R00049